Virgo

(From August 23 to September 22)

Table of Contet

The characteristics of astrological signs

What is the symbolism of your sign? His history? His qualities?

Like everyone else, you have an astrological sign determined by your date of birth. This astrological sign says a lot about you, your character, your tastes and your motivations. This Book has listed for you the characteristics of the 12 signs of the zodiac in relation to Virgo, discover all the elements to better understand your astral sign!

The Virgin: Third sign of summer, feminine, mutable Earth, ruled by Mercury.

[i]Mythology: **These are the virgin goddesses like Athena or Hestia, goddess of the home, and especially Demeter / Ceres, the mother goddess of the earth and of the harvests, sister of Zeus.**

Symbolism **and character: In the zodiac, Virgo symbolizes analysis, method, organization, classification, measurements. He is a logical, perfectionist, hardworking, practical, helpful, critical, self-conscious, detail-oriented mind. Anguished, he shows timidity and protects himself**

Obsessed with an order, he likes things to be done according to the rules of the art, but his own rules: He is the champion of advice and criticism. This sign is fussy, always has the last word, and often irritates those around him by dint of doing better than everyone else. However, his helpfulness makes him indispensable and his practicality works wonders in the face of any problem.

He has a great lack of self-confidence and finds himself relegated to the background by those who have more nerve to put themselves forward. Her modesty doesn't always help her.

Dissatisfied, frustrated, and rigid, he is an anxious person who is uncomfortable with his emotions: He hides behind a mask of coldness and control which he struggles to get rid of. The Virgin has a lot of difficulty in letting go. When he stresses, he stiffens and becomes even more perfectionist and self-critical: His demands on himself are enormous.

Devoted, he can sacrifice himself for those he loves and gives the best without complaining: The native of Virgo is never so happy as when he knows he is indispensable!

Usually discreet, he can turn into a real pipette and peddle all the gossip.

In love, this sign is modest, critical, and not very sentimental. He wants to control his instincts and everything there is human about him, especially the emotional part. Shy, self-conscious, unsure, he has a great fear of being rejected. However, it happens that, rid of her inhibitions, the so-called wise Virgo turns into a mad Virgo and becomes sexually unbridled: However, there will always be the will to keep control. A sign linked to celibacy, he often chooses to live alone, because he is able to be self-sufficient. When Virgo chooses marriage, it is for comfort or for reason.

Keywords: Purification, chastity, analysis, criticism, order, reason, division, doubt, subtraction, limitation, reserve, practice, method, detail, egoism, service, work, technique, medicine, virginity, mania, precision.

Famous Virgins : Agatha Christie - Greta Garbo - Sophia Loren - Irène Joliot-Curie - Beyonce - Cameron Diaz - Mylène Farmer - Mother Teresa - Ségolène Royal - Amy Winehouse - Adriana

Karembeu - Claudia Schiffer - Salma Hayek - Raquel Welch - Élisabeth Ire d ' England.

Richelieu - Louis XIV - Guillaume Apollinaire - Michel Drucker - Chateaubriand - Goethe - Richard Gere - Michael Jackson - Ronsard - Freddie Mercury - Keanu Reeves - Sean Connery - Henry of Wales - Stephen King - Tim Burton.

Signs affinity with the Virgin : The Taurus, the Capricorn, the Cancer, the Scorpion.

The most problematic signs with Virgo: Sagittarius, Gemini.

The additional sign of Virgo : The Fish.

If the Virgin were:

- One color: Yellow-green, gray and beige.
- A metal: Mercury
- A stone: Jasper, Tourmaline, Agate.
- An animal: The ant, the bees and the farmyard animals.
- A plant: Cereals, lavender.
- A mineral: Nickel
- Part of the body: The intestines.
- One country: Brazil, Turkey, West Indies, United States, Former Yugoslavia, Crete, Mesopotamia, Lower Silesia, State of Virginia.
- A profession: Doctor, nurse, pharmacist, accountant, surveyor, veterinarian, herbalist, expert.
- One day of the week: Wednesday
- One number: 10, 15, 27
- A note: Fa

The profile of the Virgo woman

The Virgo woman is conscientious, discreet and very pleasant to be around. She has an innate sense of organization and duty.

The native cannot consider quitting her job without everything being perfect and tidy. She is also very comfortable in society and knows how to convey her optimism. But the native is also naturally anxious, she is often afraid of doing badly, of not giving complete satisfaction to those around her, of being abandoned or unloved.

The Virgo woman prefers the shade to the light, she likes to organize a big event, but stays behind the scenes when it takes place. She can also have a little lesson-giving side that annoys her. But this is not intentional and if someone points it out to her, she will probably be very embarrassed and will try to make up for it right away.

 Because the Virgo woman has qualities of heart that are indisputable, she would not hurt a fly and loves more than anything to feel useful. She doesn't take decisions lightly and always thinks before she acts.

The Virgo woman and the men

With her, it's all white or all black: the melancholy and fragility of the Virgo woman melt men, or annoy them! For some, she represents the ideal woman, for others, she is too sensitive and anxious, thus synonymous with long boring discussions.

Either way, her suitors are up to anything for her and she won't hesitate to take advantage of it. But the Virgo woman is not mean at all and sets limits for herself.

Her real problem is that she tends to be drawn to men who don't look at her or who are too distant for her.

The Virgo woman needs a real relationship, attention and romance. When she is in love, she is quite possessive. But she would like to transform a Don Juan into a frozen lover. Obviously, it does not work and the native is then in all its forms, doubts, asks a thousand questions. To be happy in love, the Virgo woman will undoubtedly have to change this functioning and review her priorities. Happiness may just be right under his nose.

The profile of the Virgo man

The Virgo man has an important sense of duty, he likes to be of service and is pragmatic.

His concern for safety and his fear of tomorrow make him a meticulous worker who does not take his task lightly.

He is demanding and likes neither the unforeseen nor wasting his time. He will do anything to organize his life so that there is never a stone in the gear.

This character trait limits him in his ambitions: he would like to travel, discover new horizons, but prefers the comfort of his home and his reassuring habits.

The Virgo man is honest and attentive to others, he does not want to harm them in any way. Like his female counterpart, he doesn't like to put himself forward at the risk of sometimes being too discreet.

The Virgo man is, at first glance, very attached to order and to pre-established rules. On the other hand, he can suddenly be very tolerant when it comes to those around him. The social bonds and friendships that he develops are, in fact, very important to him.

Virgo man and women

In love, the Virgo man is romantic, gentlemanly and very courteous.

He is never abrupt or oppressive, and thanks to his sensitivity he can pick up on what women think. A bit shy, he will never go to a woman if he does not feel completely reassured.

He is looking for a kind and stable person like him. He is more sensitive than most men, this quality can sometimes make him vulnerable, but it also gives him a certain finesse and an ease to put himself in the other's shoes.

The native is a charming man but hard to please. When he's in love, he doesn't try to control his other half and leaves her free to come and go as she wishes.

On the other hand, he needs sincerity, comfort and family time. This is where its balance lies. The Virgo man completely plans to spend his whole life with the same woman: he is faithful, sincere, and is not a ladies' man. He is not looking for conquest but for stability.

Virgo, Earth sign, is the sixth sign of the zodiac, ruled by Mercury, in all that Mercury symbolizes of exchanges. Exchanges, Virgo already does with herself, constantly wondering if she should be a pure

spirit or just have spirit. She has no equal when it comes to
weighing the pros and cons. And this for hours. But what a soul!

The woman virgo
Salma hayek is virgo

Man virgo

HUGH GRANT is Virgo

YOUR LOVE COMPATIBILITY

Virgo woman & Virgo man

Don't believe two subjects with the same sign always get along well on the pretext that they should understand each other.

The Virgo man and the Virgo woman, however, have a fair chance of having a match. "Agreement" is the qualifier. Indeed, Virgos are right, reserved, and courteous people, and it's not in such a couple that we'll attend theatrical scenes where offensive words are exchanged.

On the other hand, these partners often lack passion and exuberance, and their union will be waves-free but can lack warmth and emotional manifestations. They're really attached to the protection and material products. This mix lacks fantasy, spontaneity, freshness. The partners may prefer to live in themselves a little closed, and will not provoke meetings.

If they don't make great efforts to isolate themselves from this life, they'll soon be bored. Their homes will be cozy, feel good, and return as much as possible.

To get out of what could seem monotonous to some, a great love for a shared ideal will have to unite our two natives. But their friendship, however calm it may be, can also make them really happy. If don't make great efforts to separate themselves from this life, they'll soon be bored.

Their homes will be cozy, feel good, and return as much as possible. To get out of what could seem monotonous to some, a great love for a shared ideal will have to unite our two natives. But their friendship, however calm it may be, can also make them really happy. If don't make great efforts to separate themselves from this life, they'll soon be bored.

To get out of what might appear to some as monotony, a great passion for a common ideal would have to bring our two natives together. But their relationship, however calm it may be, can also be enough to make them very happy.

How to seduce according to the astrological signs?

Which sign is right for you?

Astrology can help you to seduce the desired being, you just need to understand how it works and how it likes to be approached and charmed. Astro.fr gives you its secrets of seduction, no sign will resist you!

(Aries (From March 21 to April 20)

Love compatibility Virgo, Aries

What you like about the Aries: His energy, his will, his magnetism, his speed, his ingenuity, his frankness.

What makes it work: What is certain is that Aries will push you to push yourself and go where you are afraid to go. As for you, you will know how to stabilize and soften it. Your relationship is therefore possible but with a lot of effort.

What makes it not work: You will have a lot of trouble living an Aries, too impulsive, too angry. Moreover, you will judge him too inflamed and conversely, he will find you too shy, too reserved, there is little chance that it will work!

Sex-Erotic Compatibility: You have nothing in common and unless you're a crazy, saucy Virgo, it won't work!

The Aries is the most impulsive sign of the Zodiac, and this is the same feeling in his intimate! He will be more attracted by brief but intense pleasures than by long foreplay sessions, followed by the main course and dessert ...

- The Aries do not like to be refused to his ardor, so you will have to let him satisfy his impetuous impulses before being able to get some caresses, but know that once the Aries is satisfied, he will prove to be tender and affectionate to wish.

- To stimulate him, you will need to know a little how to control his ardor, while letting him believe that he remains in control of the situation. It is certainly a complicated game for beginners, but necessary for the good vitality of your couple. If you can manage to contain his appetite to make him explode when you feel the urge, then you will have an accomplished Aries!

- Signs with which Aries has the most erotic compatibility:

- Aries man: Aries, Gemini, Libra

- Aries woman: Aries, Gemini, Libra, Pisces

An astrological sign can help you understand the desired person to better seduce him. Find out what the Aries sign is hiding, the way he likes to be approached and charmed and this Aries will not be able to resist you!

The Aries are impulsive beings who often go straight to the point. So no need to chat for hours with him, the attraction between you will be largely responsible for your chemistry. Never dare to say no to an Aries because he could take it either as an affront or as a challenge!
If you want to establish a long relationship, you will always have to arouse his interest, even provoke it, to attract him in your nets. The most difficult will be to make him believe that it is always he who leads the dance!

Aries, your astral love compatibility
Aries, Astrology can help you better understand other astrological signs and thus allow you to know which signs you are the most compatible with and therefore with whom you are most likely to have your love affair working. Aries, are you ready to find out which other zodiac sign is right for you?

Aries(From March 21 to April 20)
The fiery temperament of Aries goes well with the fire signs precisely, such as Aries , Leo and Sagittarius , because they

are on the same wavelength and the intensity that animates them can make beautiful sparks. Small flat for Sagittarius who may not find the beautiful declarations of love they are so fond of, because the Aries is not very talkative and he will much prefer to act to show his feelings, than to make long romantic speeches .

The air signs: Gemini , Libra and Aquarius , will also find a beautiful complementarity in Aries , insofar as the latter's energy will be a stimulant to establish projects for two and to break the routine that greatly restricts the signs of 'air. Passion will therefore be at the rendezvous, but beware of slippages that could cause a stubborn grudge!

With the earth signs: Taurus , Virgo and Capricorn , the understanding will be less certain because these signs need stability and understanding, while Aries often acts on impulsivity and in a very spontaneous way. The relationship can be viable if the Aries feels able to open up and communicate, but you should know that the Aries hates compromise, even those that seem feasible at first glance ...

On the other hand, with the water signs: Cancer , Scorpio and Pisces , the relationship will be difficult in the long term! Even if the beginnings seem promising, especially under the covers, once the passion has died down, the nature of these signs will return at a gallop and demonstrate such a difference in their expectations that one of the two, if not both, will come out greatly frustrated!

The Virgin can show great ambivalence about his sexuality, and if by nature, it has a quite introverted temperament, however, it can be as insatiable as a harpy. So you can be dealing with a totally different person, it will depend greatly on the sexual attraction that will reign between you.

Usually, it will take a little while before you see her break free from the shackles, they impose on herself, but she can quickly become fiery and leave you speechless in the face of her powerful boundless energy.

It is appropriate to please Virgo, so it's up to you to find the locks that will make her inhibitions jump. Know, however, that if she is disappointed with your antics, she will close in on herself.

Signs with which Virgo has the most erotic compatibility:

Virgo man: Taurus, Cancer, Leo, Virgo, Capricorn, Pisces

Virgo woman: Taurus, Virgo, Libra, Scorpio, Capricorn, Aquarius

How to seduce a Virgo?
An astrological sign can help you understand the desired person to better seduce him. Find out what the Virgo sign hides, the way they like to be approached and charmed and this Virgo will not be able to resist you!

Virgin (From August 23 to September 22)

The Virgin you will seem perhaps a little stiff and difficult to address, but under his cold exterior hides a personality just waiting to explode! If you manage to instill passion between you, Virgo will lose restraint and let go, to offer you the best of themselves.

It will therefore be for you to always animate this spark so that the Virgin does not lose in intensity. Also know that she is very receptive to nice statements, but on the other hand, she hates fine talkers.

Virgo, your astral love compatibility

Virgo, Astrology can help you better understand other astrological signs and thus let you know which signs you are the most compatible with and therefore with whom you are most likely to have your love affair working. Virgo, are you ready to find out which other zodiac sign is right for you?

Virgin (From August 23 to September 22)

With the other earth signs (Taurus, Virgo, Capricorn), you find yourself completely in your way of seeing things, and in your common passion to establish constructive projects for your future. Reason motivates you and you can very well have a fulfilling and long relationship, provided that the routine is sometimes broken.

Water signs (Cancer, Scorpio, Pisces) can give Virgo the proofs of love they need to feel secure in their relationship. The relationship will certainly not be very passionate, but this is not what Virgo seeks, who rather favors comfort and complicity. They will thus evolve in confidence and fulfillment.

The Virgin is impressed by the boundless energy of the fire signs (Aries, Leo and Sagittarius), but it does not take long sail! Yet a little madness would do a little too calculating Virgo a lot of good. The fire signs don't give her the security she seeks, however, and she might become a little too suspicious and suffer from this disrespect.

The air signs (Gemini, Libra, Aquarius) are a real puzzle for you! You don't understand their light-heartedness and it hurts you to have to run after proofs of love. The relationship can work if you have an air sign ascendant and are willing to accept their needs for freedom. Ideal for short relationships, but not too long ...

Love compatibility Virgo, Virgo

What pleases you about the Virgin: Her method, her depth of mind, her calm and reasoned side, her uprightness of mind.

What makes it work: On the same wavelength, you are quite similar in ideas and principles of life which can only bring you closer. So, you have the same desires, the same goals and your relationship can be very balanced.

What makes it not work: You often tend to seek the little beast and you keep tickling yourselves. So in the long run, your relationship can be compromised. It's up to you to be less critical and demanding!

Sex-erotic compatibility: 'It can do it' as they say even if you can alternate periods of passion, wisdom or chastity.

Love compatibility Virgo, Taurus

What you like about Taurus: Its reassuring, calm, calm aspect. His sensitivity, his taste for life, his even humor, his tone of voice.

What makes it work: Both Earth signs, you're almost made in the same mold and you get along like thieves. So, all the elements are there for you to form a balanced couple.

What makes it not work: Your only problem will surely be a lack of exchanges or communication; however, you will always manage to find common ground and to listen. Let the time and the experience of life for two take places.

Sex-Erotic Compatibility: While you don't have the same expectations, you still pretty much stay on the same page.

•	The Taurus loves sex and pleasure lies in the penetration. He will probably be less inclined to foreplay but he will be able to satisfy you without any problem for a whole night as his devotion to you will be great.

He is not resistant to caresses during the act and will even be very happy if you show initiative during your lovemaking, on the other hand, if you refuse him or that you do not let him satisfy all his desires, he might turn away from you.

We know the Taurus is very possessive, therefore, if you plan to look elsewhere, it will hurt him to the greatest extent, but if you give your all to him, he will certainly know how to make you a sexually fulfilled person.

Signs with which Taurus has the most erotic compatibility:

Taurus man : Taurus, Virgo, Libra, Sagittarius, Pisces

Taurus woman: Taurus, Virgo, Scorpio, Pisces

How to seduce a Taurus?
An astrological sign can help you understand the desired person to better seduce him. Find out what the Taurus sign hides, the way it likes to be approached and charmed and this Taurus will not be able to resist you!
Taurus
Taurus (From April 21 to May 20)
The Taurus is generally very tactile, he likes hugs, melee, so if you want to seduce him, nothing could be easier, you just have to get into his game! Obviously, a touch of resistance on your part will strengthen your relationship and further pique his interest. The Taurus is also very possessive and it is advisable not to play with him too much on this subject, at the risk of seeing him move away definitively from you.

Finally, know that Taurus prefers long stories, he greatly appreciates hesitant beginnings, filled with mutual desire, and will therefore be upset by too much impatience on your part.

Taurus, your astral love compatibility
Taurus, Astrology can help you better understand other astrological signs and thus allow you to know which signs you are the most compatible with and therefore with whom you are most likely to have your love affair working. Taurus, are you ready to find out which other zodiac sign is best for you?

Taurus (From April 21 to May 20)

The Taurus is naturally attracted to water signs (Cancer, Scorpio, Pisces) as his love needs will be understood by those very sensual and generous signs. Their relationship can even become very close-knit as long as they share everything and are always honest with each other, if so, then Taurus' demands will always be met!

A beautiful bond can appear with the earth signs (Taurus, Virgo and Capricorn), because they share the same desires and the same ambitions for the future! The problem could however come from their relation to money and from the investments that each plan to make alone in his corner, instead of sharing it with the other. As long as communication is on, this problem shouldn't be insurmountable!

With the fire signs (Aries , Leo and Sagittarius), Taurus will be more than troubled, as the constant changing needs of the fire signs greatly alter their deep nature, which yearns for more tranquility! For the relationship to be viable, the Taurus would have to use his great energy to constantly surprise his partner or that the fire signs curb their nomadic instincts, which is not a given!

No cordial agreement with the air signs (Gemini, Libra and Aquarius) but a relationship rather based on compromises, where each one tries to put his first interests before those of the other. The possessiveness of Taureans will be a brake on the air signs that need to feel free from all constraints. The Taurus will suffer from not feeling loved the way they want.

(Gemini (From May 21 to June 20)

Love compatibility Virgo, Gemini

What appeals to you about Gemini: His open-mindedness, his need for novelty, his originality, his sense of analysis, his adaptability, his gestures, his words.

What makes it work: Both Ruled by Mercury, planet of exchanges, you can get along well and you can multiply initiatives and projects.

What makes it not work: You don't communicate in the same way and you will often face a lot of disagreements. In addition, the Gemini sign will find you too rigid for its liking and you too dissipated. There is little chance that it will work!

Sex-erotic compatibility: Not having too many expectations, you will not be really disappointed, but you will not have the same desires.

The Gemini is a free enough sign that it is unnecessary constraints, that's why he likes to make love, in any form whatsoever! He likes to experiment but will just as well be content with a good classic, he has small domineering inclinations, but also enjoys being dominated ...

 The important thing will lie in the personality of his partner, who must be as generous and open as him, otherwise, the Gemini will feel trapped in a routine and a boredom that he particularly loathes.

Imagination is a motor for him, so you can use and abuse your creativity, he will be drawn to you all the more. And the more you stimulate his mind, the more he will reward you!

Signs with which Gemini has the most erotic compatibility:

Gemini man: Aries, Gemini, Leo, Sagittarius

Gemini woman: Aries, Gemini, Leo, Libra, Sagittarius

How to seduce a Gemini?
An astrological sign can help you understand the desired person to better seduce him. Find out what the Gemini sign is hiding, the way it likes to be approached and charmed and this Gemini will not be able to resist you!

Gemini (From May 21 to June 20)

The Gemini loves to communicate, to transmit, to discover the tastes of each one, it is then easy to seduce him especially if you have a lot of eloquence. He will expect complete loyalty from you and will not understand complex personalities, full of inhibitions and modesty.

You will have more chance to seduce him in the evening because he is a person who has a very active social life and who loves to party. On the other hand, you will always have to find something to feed your discussions and arouse his interest so that he does not tire of you and sails towards other more attractive personalities.

Gemini, your astral love compatibility

Gemini, Astrology can help you better understand other astrological signs and thus let you know which signs you are most compatible with and therefore with whom you are most likely to have your love affair working. Gemini, are you ready to find out which other zodiac sign is right for you?

Gemini (From May 21 to June 20)

Fire signs (Aries, Leo and Sagittarius) can establish a fiery and powerful romantic relationship with Gemini, as they share a strong desire for discovery and perpetual action in their relationship. The Gemini need to express themselves both verbally and physically and fire signs are quite adept at channeling this generous influx. The Gemini calmer will however need to be more in seduction and daring face these very greedy fire signs in thrills.

With the air signs (Gemini, Libra, Aquarius), osmosis is possible and even very deep, provided that communication takes precedence over their need for autonomy. The quality of their exchanges will be exceptional if mutual respect is maintained, and above all, if they leave space for each other's freedom, the basis for the development of air signs.

Water signs (Cancer, Scorpio, Pisces) may bring a bit of trouble to Gemini, because they are rarely expressive, much more cerebral, they prevent Gemini from knowing with certainty what we are expected from him. Unless a very strong physical attraction binds them both together, Gemini will hardly be able to feel loved the way they want them to, and water signs will be too overwhelmed by Gemini's abundance of emotions.

For earth signs (Taurus, Virgo, Capricorn), Gemini is far too articulate and their need for freedom is a constant anxiety for earth signs, which are very possessive. The Gemini can be stifled if it feels too much grip, it will go away without looking back. This relationship could work, but with a lot of compromise and mutual trust, which is very hard for both of them ...

(Cancer (From June 21 to July 22)

Love compatibility Virgo, Cancer

What you like about Cancer: His gentleness, his empathy, his sense of values and family, his need for stability.

What Makes It Work: While not being in the same universe, you can find some waiting grounds to make your relationship work, but it won't be easy.

What makes it not work: If the two of you are attached to your habits and values, you don't have the same outlook on life and it can damage your relationship. Thus, you will have to learn to communicate and especially to overcome your differences.

Sex-Erotic Compatibility: You will quickly feel frustrated as much as the other and there is little chance that you will agree.

The Cancer is one of the most tactile signs of the Zodiac, caresses therefore have a preference, but it will also be very affectionate with you. On the other hand, it is a sign that will probably take a little time to fully reveal itself to you, because he needs to feel confident and to know his partner a minimum.

Even if he will never admit it to you, Cancer prefers to be the dominated rather than the dominant, the key is to do it with a lot of tenderness and gentleness, and if you succeed, you will probably have his approval to try everything. whatever you see fit.

Finally, know that Cancer needs to feel that feelings are shared otherwise, he can close in on himself and only offer you a mediocre performance, at best ...

Signs with which Cancer has the most erotic compatibility:

Cancer man: Cancer, Libra, Capricorn, Aquarius, Pisces

Cancer woman: Cancer, Virgo, Libra, Aquarius

How to seduce a Cancer?
An astrological sign can help you understand the desired person to better seduce him. Find out what the Cancer sign is

hiding, how he likes to be approached and charmed and this Cancer will not be able to resist you!

Cancer (From June 21 to July 22)

The Cancer needs to be reassured, to feel that we love for what it is, it will certainly be very receptive to the fine words and to persons attached to family values. You will seduce him by the gentle manner, because it is a sign who does not appreciate too much abruptness and prefers the compliments and the attention that one gives him.

Know how to be protective and show him that you are concerned about his well-being and his problems, then there will be no obstacle to him opening up completely to you.

Cancer, your astral love compatibility

Cancer, Astrology can help you better understand other astrological signs and thus allow you to know which signs you are most compatible with and therefore with whom you are most likely to have your love affair working. Cancer, are you ready to find out which other zodiac sign is best for you?

Cancer (From June 21 to July 22)

The earth signs (Taurus, Virgo, Capricorn) are good allies to meet the emotional needs of Cancer. If the earth signs act with caution and tact, they can count on Cancer to give them all their love. Their development will happen naturally and couple projects will be a driving force for their personal enrichment.

With the water signs (Cancer, Scorpio and Pisces) the agreement will be good if the dialogue remains honest, because Cancerians hate being disappointed and deceived, and good communication is generally the key to a successful relationship. Between water signs, understanding is mutual, and for the relationship to work better, Cancer should not feel dominated, but rather in balance.

With the fire signs (Aries, Leo and Sagittarius) Cancer is in constant questioning about its relationship, it is not reassured by the fiery behavior of the fire signs. The Cancer needs being questioned, to be shown the love we feel for him, he does not live-in passion but within reason, the opposite signs of fire!

There remain the air signs (Gemini, Libra, Aquarius), with whom the relationship will be very lively! These signs are crazy about freedom, while Cancer is generally rather enamored of its cocoon. This couple will have a hard time living in harmony, because their respective needs will always be out of balance with each other, if they are really in love with each other, they will have to find the right rhythm.

(Lion (From July 23 to August 22)

Love compatibility Virgo, Leo

What you like about Leo: His aura, his sense of synthesis, his way of moving forward in life, his panache, his determination.

What makes it work: You will know how to structure each other. Thus, the Leo will constantly push you to surpass yourself and you will know how to reason with it, moderate it.

What makes that it cannot work: Rather discreet, you will sometimes have a hard time living the egocentricity of the Leo who often needs to bring everything back to him. Being in the opposite direction and in the negation of yourself, your couple will have a hard time enduring time.

Sex-erotic compatibility: It can work like none at all, here it is above all a story of feelings.

The Leo likes to be made love to him, and even more when it is done well! If he finds a powerful partner in you, he will let go completely, especially if he feels a very strong physical attraction for you.

He will be sensitive to beautiful places and very attractive people, especially if they are good at making him lustful!

Everything matters to the Leo, from the first minute to the last, every detail will be important and will influence his behavior with you, so you have the cards in hand to make this Lion prey at your mercy.

Signs with which Leo has the most erotic compatibility:

Leo man : Gemini, Leo, Libra, Pisces

Leo woman: Gemini, Leo, Virgo, Scorpio, Pisces

How to seduce a Leo?

An astrological sign can help you understand the desired person to better seduce him. Find out what the Leo sign hides, how he likes to be approached and charmed and this Leo will not be able to resist you!

Lion (From July 23 to August 22)

The Lion 's are spectators rather actors, they love you and deceive them that the values they feel so appreciated at their true value. However, you will need to have a strong character and also be someone who is a little out of the ordinary. Flattering him will be the best way to achieve your ends, but it will have to be done with finesse, because the Leo is anything but naive.

If you give him all the attention he requires, then he will be demonstrative with you, but know that, in any case, he will be the one who will let himself be carried by the relationship.

Leo, your astral love compatibility

Leo, Astrology can help you better understand other astrological signs and thus let you know which signs you are the most compatible with and therefore with whom you are most likely to have your love affair working. Leo, are you ready to find out which other zodiac sign is right for you?

Lion (From July 23 to August 22)

The fire signs (Aries, Leo and Sagittarius) are, in general, quite compatible with Leo, as they are both in greatness and energy. The need for novelty is a driving force that they share, as is the desire to make projects and to be in constant search of intellectual as well as sensual satisfaction.

With the air signs (Gemini - Libra and Aquarius), Leo can also aim for a beautiful relationship which will be above all based on originality and play. Leo likes to be surprised in Love, and who better than the signs of air to offer him a relationship that is always on the move and full of twists and turns. The Lion will always respond present as long as we let him breathe!

The Leo is not content with the good, he wants the best! This little sin of pride undermines his relationship with the earth signs (Taurus, Virgo and Capricorn), because the latter are rather on the reserve and do not appreciate the impetuosity very much. For their relationship to work, the two must bring to the other what is lacking, and thus manage to balance this relationship all in compromise.

With the water signs (Cancer, Scorpio and Pisces) the Leo risks getting bored, trapped in a straitjacket far too calm for his liking. The water signs are a little too posed for the Leo who seeks a loving dynamic in constant working order. The relationship can survive if one of the two lets go of their inclinations for the other, but the balance will never be even.

Love compatibility Virgo, Libra

What you like about Libra: His sensitivity, his taste for art, finesse, his wit, his sense of communication, his need for balance.

What makes that it can work: You can create a stable universe, enriching and bathed in harmony because both aspiring to peace and well-being. So your couple can walk perfectly.

What makes that it cannot work: You will sometimes have a hard time understanding the indecisions of Libra who, although wanting to commit, will have difficulty taking the plunge, just as this last sign will hardly live your critical and demanding side.

Sex-Erotic Compatibility: If the beginnings can be nice over time, your relationship and your seduction will wear out!

The balance is probably one of the most difficult to fill because signs his legendary indecisiveness and his great need to explore doing it often feels misunderstood or unloved. You will therefore have a lot to do to satisfy her, but if you play the affection card and take your time, you should manage to awaken her sensuality and make her sparkling!

The balance is not a big fan of short relationships, she prefers a largely full of sweetness married life that will allow him to deepen his sexuality with confidence.

She will accept dominating as well as being dominated, but it will be up to you to adapt to her pace!

Signs with which Libra has the most erotic compatibility:

Libra man : Aries, Gemini, Cancer , Virgo, Libra, Sagittarius

Libra woman: Aries, Taurus, Cancer, Leo, Libra, Sagittarius

How to seduce a Libra?

An astrological sign can help you understand the desired person to better seduce him. Find out what the Libra sign hides, the way it likes to be approached and charmed and this Libra won't be able to resist you!

Balance (From September 23 to October 23)

The balance is by definition uncertain, you should therefore exercise patience and persuasion to achieve your goals. The Libra appreciate people playful, energetic, but also stable, then do not seem too pushy or versatile, risk of seeing it away from you quickly.

She will be patient before giving her all because she needs to feel confident, so expect to have a lot of talking together and having to reassure her about your feelings and intentions.

Scorpio, your astral love compatibility

Scorpio, Astrology can help you better understand other astrological signs and thus allow you to know which signs you are most compatible with and therefore with whom you are most likely to have your love affair working. Scorpio, are you ready to find out which other zodiac sign is right for you?

Scorpio (October 24 to November 22)

With water signs like him (Cancer, Scorpio and Pisces), Scorpio manages to find a balance because their desires are equivalent. Both intellectually and physically, Scorpio can flourish, and if they feel in a healthy relationship, Scorpio will give all their sensuality and attention.

The earth signs (Taurus, Virgo and Capricorn) are a good arrangement as long as Scorpio is not subject to the strong character of the earth sign. If the relationship plays diplomacy and communicates well on both sides, the understanding can be very complementary. On the other hand, if the two stick to their positions, the relationship can quickly turn sour and resentment!

Fun will be the watchword with the air signs (Gemini, Libra and Aquarius), but it will only last for a while. Too much dissatisfaction will win over the Scorpio who will never be reassured by a sign of air too busy to live in the moment. For this relationship to work, both parties need to play their cards right on the table and be irreproachable, but is it possible?

The fire signs (Aries, Leo and Sagittarius) are far too superficial for the Scorpio in search of love stability. The passion at the beginning will only be window dressing, because when expectations are not met, Scorpio will fail to breathe new life into their relationship. Communication will be a major problem and their constant competitiveness will bring them to ruin.

Libra, your astral love compatibility

Libra, Astrology can help you better understand other astrological signs and thus let you know which signs you are the most compatible with and therefore with whom you are most likely to have your love affair working. Libra, are you ready to find out which other zodiac sign is best for you?

Balance (From September 23 to October 23)

The air signs (Gemini, Libra, Aquarius) have her preference, because she finds herself in their joviality and their need to be on the move. The Libra is attracted to a quality love, a strong and satisfying love, she does not feel suffocated by the signs of air and can thus give all its measure and its cheerfulness to this relationship.

With the signs of fire (Aries, Leo and Sagittarius) she finds fascinating and passionate affinities, but in the long term, this may tire her, because Libra also seeks stability and balance in her relationship. If the fire signs manage to secure her, she will let go without restraint and give her whole person.

The earth signs (Taurus, Virgo and Capricorn) are a little too predictable for her liking! The balance is very indecisive by nature, she is struggling to make choices while earth signs are in absolute control. The situations then risk turning into a drama and for a Libra who hates conflict, it will be very difficult to live!

Nothing will be easy with the water signs (Cancer, Scorpio and Pisces) because the apparent tranquility of the latter, in fact hides a deep feeling of insecurity that Libra cannot reassure.

The balance will miss because the water signs are not living in the moment but in continuity, their expectations are too different to be able to give something meaningful over time.

Love compatibility Virgo, Scorpio

What appeals to you about Scorpio: Their sex appeal, their mysterious and secretive mind, their need to learn, to understand.

What makes it work: You were made to get along, there is no doubt. One knowing how to appease the other and the other knowing how to bring him to unknown lands. Your couple will not be short of chilies and twists.

What makes that it cannot work: The repeated crises of the Scorpio, its prickly, even cynical side towards which you will be able to defend yourself perfectly with your critical and acerbic spirit. Learn to respect yourself if you want it to work.

Sex-erotic compatibility: Astrology wants you to be complementary and this is not wrong since Scorpio knows how to bring out in you all that is most sensual!

The Scorpio is a fine strategist, because he will allow himself to be charmed in order to better conquer you later. Do not be fooled by their apparent shyness or passivity, Scorpio is a sign that in the end will like to dominate you.

So expect to have to abandon yourself to him, because the more you are submissive and the more his pleasure will increase tenfold, providing you at the same time, unforgettable moments.

To achieve your ends with a Scorpio, you will need to establish a gradual rhythm where you will gradually succumb to him, so the pleasure will be prolonged and it can last over time to initiate a long relationship between you.

Signs with which Scorpio has the most erotic compatibility:

Scorpio man: Taurus, Leo, Virgo, Scorpio, Aquarius   Scorpio woman: Scorpio, Aquarius

How to seduce a Scorpio?
An astrological sign can help you understand the desired person to better seduce him. Find out what the Scorpio sign hides, how he likes to be approached and charmed and this Scorpio will not be able to resist you!

Scorpio (October 24 to November 22)

To seduce a Scorpio, you will have to prove to them that you have something that they lack! Everything will therefore be in seduction and persuasion; you will have to highlight your strengths and you should especially not play on your possible resemblance but rather on your complementarity.

The Scorpio can be very patient, and make you wait a long time before agreeing to you, but know that once convinced, he can prove to be a very pleasant partner.

Scorpio, your astral love compatibility

Scorpio, Astrology can help you better understand other astrological signs and thus allow you to know which signs you are most compatible with and therefore with whom you are most likely to have your love affair working. Scorpio, are you ready to find out which other zodiac sign is right for you?

Scorpio (October 24 to November 22)

With water signs like him (Cancer, Scorpio and Pisces), Scorpio manages to find a balance because their desires are equivalent. Both intellectually and physically, Scorpio can flourish, and if they feel in a healthy relationship, Scorpio will give all their sensuality and attention.

The earth signs (Taurus, Virgo and Capricorn) are a good arrangement as long as Scorpio is not subject to the strong character of the earth sign. If the relationship plays diplomacy and communicates well on both sides, the understanding can be very complementary. On the other hand, if the two stick to their positions, the relationship can quickly turn sour and resentment!

Fun will be the watchword with the air signs (Gemini, Libra and Aquarius), but it will only last for a while. Too much dissatisfaction will win over the Scorpio who will never be reassured by a sign of air too busy to live in the moment. For this relationship to work, both parties need to play their cards right on the table and be irreproachable, but is it possible?

The fire signs (Aries, Leo and Sagittarius) are far too superficial for the Scorpio in search of love stability. The passion at the beginning will only be window dressing, because when expectations are not met, Scorpio will fail to breathe new life into their relationship. Communication will be a major problem and their constant competitiveness will bring them to ruin.

(Sagittarius (From November 23 to December 22)

Love compatibility Virgo, Sagittarius

What you like about Sagittarius: His generosity of soul and heart, his need to move, to break the monotony, so everything you don't know how to do!

What makes it work: You get along really well, and Sagittarius makes you evolve and view life in a more positive way. Upside down, you get to calm it down, make it more realistic.

Which means that it cannot work: You will have a hard time living the need for adventures of this Fire sign to constantly conquer an ideal, just as it will have difficulty staying wisely by your side! Learn to accept everyone's differences!

Sex-erotic compatibility: This Fire sign does not lack ideas to ignite the powder, but you still have to be receptive!

The Sagittarius is not too difficult, he will be carried away by the situation and give what is best if you really buff. He is someone who greatly appreciates foreplay and the more he is satisfied on this point, the more it will awaken his sensuality.

You should also know that when the Sagittarius is in love, he gives without counting, listens to his partner, and likes to establish a beautiful intimate bond, on the other hand, if he is not inspired, he can simply be a belt. for a long time without batting an eyelid.

The Sagittarius also appreciates the fair reports, he will not appreciate to feel dominated as he will not like to be dominant.

Signs with which Sagittarius has the most erotic compatibility:

Sagittarius man: Gemini, Libra, Sagittarius, Pisces

Sagittarius woman: Taurus, Gemini, Libra, Sagittarius, Pisces

How to seduce a Sagittarius?

An astrological sign can help you understand the desired person to better seduce him. Find out what the Sagittarius sign is hiding, how they like to be approached and charmed and this Sagittarius will not be able to resist you!

Sagittarius (From November 23 to December 22)

The Sagittarius needs someone to do the dream, so you find things at home which will fascinate and arouse his interest. Think outside the box, bet on romance and you will touch it right in the heart!

Nevertheless, know that the Sagittarius hates disappointments, if he learns that you lied to him, he will probably turn his back on you without regret, so it is still best to play your card on the table from the start with him.

Sagittarius, your astral love compatibility

Sagittarius, Astrology can help you better understand other astrological signs and thus allow you to know which signs you are most compatible with and therefore with whom you are most likely to have your love affair working. Sagittarius, are you ready to find out which other zodiac sign is right for you?

Sagittarius (From November 23 to December 22)

The Sagittarius is found in other fire signs (Aries, Leo and Sagittarius), although their expectations are slightly different. The Sagittarius is more in pure love, it gives a lot of enthusiasm and gaiety if he feels like it tickles and that makes him feel alive! The fire signs live their passion in the moment and give everything, as long as they are constantly stimulated.

With the air signs (Gemini, Libra and Aquarius), the Sagittarius will show a boundless freedom of expression because he will feel listened to by the very communicative air signs. On the other hand, he will have to be the one in control to be able to give his full confidence, and this is not easy with the air signs by nature very independent and free, but the Sagittarius is able to achieve it with discretion.!

The water signs (Cancer, Scorpio and Pisces) are a double-edged attraction for the Sagittarius who feels close to them by their sentimentality, but far away by their lack of expressiveness. In the long term, this relationship will prove to be very difficult for the Sagittarius who will never stop having to prove his love and wait in return for proofs of affection which will be slow in coming.

The earth signs (Taurus, Virgo and Capricorn), are too far-sighted for the Sagittarius who needs a little touch of madness to feel alive. The watchword in this relationship will be negotiation, they will have to give up a lot of their convictions for the relationship to last over time, but Sagittarius can hardly accept being constantly restrained without obtaining satisfaction in return.

Love compatibility Virgo, Capricorn

What appeals to you about Capricorn: His desire to stabilize, his determination, his reliability, his sense of responsibility.

What makes it work: You get along really well and you have a lot in common. Thus, you can form a solid couple who can evolve over time while going through hardships!

What makes it not work: Your biggest problem is the lack of communication, the need to maintain certain habits. So over time your life will become like a kind of ritual. Try to get out of this context!

Sex-erotic compatibility: You have the same expectations and just for that your relationship will stick!

The Capricorn is generally in agreement with himself regarding his sexuality. Not too much extravagance to expect from him, but rather an evolving sensuality based on a beautiful bond.

The Capricorn can think outside the box, however, but on the condition that you take matters into your own hands without him realizing it. It's a tough game, but one that can pay off, especially if you like to spice things up a bit!

The Capricorn will bring security and affection, but do not expect a whirlwind of passion with him stability still prevail.

Signs with which Capricorn has the most erotic compatibility:

Capricorn man: Virgo, Capricorn, Pisces

Capricorn woman: Cancer, Virgo, Capricorn

How to seduce a Capricorn?

An astrological sign can help you understand the desired person to better seduce him. Find out what the Capricorn sign hides, how he likes to be approached and charmed and this Capricorn will not be able to resist you!

Capricorn (From December 23 to January 19)

The Capricorn is not a great original, he likes simplicity and especially serenity. No need therefore to dazzle him with fanciful behavior and excesses of all kinds, he will not be impressed, on the contrary. Rather, bet on coherent words, a quiet personality and cultural outings to achieve your goals.

 Rest assured, the Capricorn also knows how to bring a little grain of madness in his life, but he will not show it to you until he is one hundred percent certain of your intentions, so be patient!

Capricorn, your astral love compatibility

Capricorn, Astrology can help you better understand other astrological signs and thus let you know which signs you are the most compatible with and therefore with whom you are most likely to have your love affair working. Capricorn, are you ready to find out which other zodiac sign is best for you?

Capricorn (From December 23 to January 19)

The earth signs (Taurus, Virgo and Capricorn) have great affinities even if there are a few distinctions between them. Indeed, if the Capricorn does not feel loved, he becomes defeatist and his relationship gives him a lot of concerns. But generally, the similar expectations of earth signs provide a stability and clarity that Capricorns particularly fond of.

The water signs (Cancer, Scorpio and Pisces) assure Capricorn tenderness and balance, and in return, it gives them security and emotional solidity. Their complementarity can lead to good relationships if the communication is clear and the problems are raised diplomatically. The Capricorn will feel fulfilled and calmed by the very poised nature water signs.

With the air signs (Gemini, Libra, Aquarius), the relationship is difficult to stabilize because the expectations are diametrically opposed. The Capricorn who seeks peace of mind will not be reassured by the irrational temperament of air signs, nor will they find themselves in their need for escape and sociability. Compromises are to be expected so that everyone finds noon at their doorstep.

The fire signs (Aries, Leo and Sagittarius) are far too exuberant for the Capricorn who loves gentleness and seriousness. Passion can last a while and fill Capricorn, but the relationship will be doomed if both parties don't make some changes in the way they think about a long-term relationship.

(Aquarius (From January 20 to February 18)

Love compatibility Virgo, Aquarius

What you like about Aquarius: His human qualities, his sense of innovation, his need for discovery and novelty.

What makes that it can work: You will communicate on ideas, modes of thoughts, it is one of the strong points of your couple which will allow you to have a minimum of exchanges per key.

What makes it not work: You will not always feel comfortable with an Aquarius because you will not have the same centers of interest and your exchanges will be by touch or in a roundabout way, not ideal for considering the long term.

Sex-erotic compatibility: In a love-friendship mode, you will not find fulfillment, it is a relationship to be taken as a moment of minute tenderness and not otherwise!

The Aquarius is like moods: changing! It will therefore be difficult for you to tame him, but you should, on the other hand, not get bored with him. Sometimes gentle as a lamb, sometimes wild like a lion, you will never know which way to dance!

Very focused on games and novelty, Aquarius will certainly know how to draw you into scenarios straight out of his fertile imagination, and he will know how to initiate you as well as learn from you!

Know that Aquarius sees all of this as fun, if you are too classic or cerebral, they won't bother you for very long!

Signs with which Aquarius has the most erotic compatibility:

Aquarius man: Cancer, Virgo, Scorpio, Aquarius

Aquarius woman: Cancer, Scorpio, Aquarius

How to seduce an Aquarius?

An astrological sign can help you understand the desired person to better seduce him. Find out what the Aquarius sign hides, the way it likes to be approached and charmed and this Aquarius will not be able to resist you!

Aquarius (From January 20 to February 18)

If you want to seduce an Aquarius, you will surely have to think outside the box and bet on originality and non-conformism. The Aquarius is a rebel at heart, he will appreciate dreamers, freedom-loving and independent figures, although generally he appreciates most people.

On the other hand, do not hope to tame it or make it change, because Aquarius will always be true to itself, and if you do not adapt to his personality, it is better not to persevere in seduction ...

Aquarius, your astral love compatibility

Aquarius, Astrology can help you better understand other astrological signs and thus allow you to know which signs you are most compatible with and therefore with whom you are most likely to have your love affair working. Aquarius, are you ready to find out which other zodiac sign is right for you?

Aquarius (From January 20 to February 18)

The air signs (Gemini, Libra and Aquarius) bring a promise of harmonious love for the Aquarius who seeks powerful and complicit exchanges. The romantic relationship will be tender but embellished with a little touch of madness which is necessary for the enrichment of the couple. If the areas of freedom are respected, the relationship will be balanced and lasting.

With the earth signs (Taurus, Virgo, Capricorn) the mix can be daring but viable, provided the Aquarius feels free to move around. If doubts arise, then it will be necessary to base the relation on a clear communication, otherwise, each one will remain holed in his corner while waiting for the other to take the first step. And it can go on for years ...

The signs of fire (Aries, Leo and Sagittarius), take Aquarius to countries that they would not have dared to cross alone, but after the euphoria of the moment, the return to reality is often brutal for the fervent Aquarius. stability. The relationship is however possible and very promising if the Aquarius allows himself to be led without restraint by the fiery temperament of the fire signs.

Relationships with the water signs (Cancer, Scorpio and Pisces) are far too boring for Aquarius to find real fulfillment. The Aquarius is moving forward, it will not look back and make a life in the short- and long-term projects. Water signs live in the past, nostalgia is their engine to move forward, a consideration that Aquarius will find difficult to accept, and which will put a lot of distance between them.

Love compatibility Virgo, Pisces

What you like about Pisces: Its skin-deep sensitivity, its sensuality, its romanticism, its softness, its altruistic side.

What makes it work: You attract yourself as you repel yourself. However, the Pisces has the art and the manner to cheer you up and very gently, he knows how to bring you towards a rather nice relationship.

What makes that it cannot work: Your contradictions, the irrationality of Pisces, its lack of accuracy and conversely, your severe side, too straight, too maniac, too much!

Sex-erotic compatibility: If the feeling passes, you will not be disappointed, however be careful because we can even say that it is a sign that you can have in the skin!

The Fish will say yes to everything, as far as we asked! So do not expect him to take the initiatives in love, he will do nothing, on the other hand, he will comply with your slightest desires and that with pleasure.

He will lend himself more to gentleness and delicacy than to lovemaking imbued with passion or even a minimum of bestiality, moreover this may outright prevent him from finding pleasure in it.

He can sometimes be so passive, that even if his sex life did not suit him, he would do nothing to change it ... Some people appreciate malleable partners like him, but others will struggle with his lack of initiative.

Signs with which Pisces has the most erotic compatibility:

Pisces man: Aries, Taurus, Leo, Sagittarius, Pisces

Pisces woman: Taurus, Cancer, Leo, Virgo, Sagittarius, Capricorn, Pisces

How to seduce a Pisces?

An astrological sign can help you understand the desired person to better seduce him. Find out what the Pisces sign hides, the way he likes to be approached and charmed and this Pisces won't be able to resist you!

Pisces (From February 19 to March 20)

The Fish is one of the nicest signs of the zodiac, but it is also the most elusive! You will therefore have great difficulty in attracting it in your nets, and some tricks will surely be required to achieve your ends. Let him believe that he was the one who caught you, when you've been strutting around in front of him all evening. In short, arousing his desire will surely be a fruitful approach.

Also know that a little firmness will not be useless, because the Pisces is quite malleable, however, always go there with a smile, it will be the best tactic to charm him!

Pisces, your astral love compatibility

Pisces, Astrology can help you better understand other astrological signs and thus let you know which signs you are the most compatible with and therefore with whom you are most likely to have your love affair working. Pisces, are you ready to find out which other zodiac sign is best for you?

Pisces (From February 19 to March 20)

The water signs (Cancer, Scorpio, Pisces) obviously have a lot of attractions for the Pisces greedy in shared emotions. They conceive of love in a very cerebral way, and their peacefulness generally emerges a soft and complicit relationship. Only Scorpio will be able to find Pisces a little too affectionate for their liking, but that won't be a major problem!

With the earth signs (Taurus, Virgo and Capricorn), Pisces can form a balanced relationship only if the earth signs do not suffocate them with their possessiveness and control. Their complementarities are numerous and the Pisces will gladly leave the reins of the relationship to his partner if he feels safe and invested with another responsibility just as important in his eyes.

The air signs (Gemini, Libra and Aquarius) attract the Pisces, but some disillusions can come to mar this beautiful meeting, because the Pisces needs directives to move forward, something that the air signs are not too able to. give him. Arrangements will therefore be made so that Pisces feels good in his day-to-day relationship.

Fire signs (Aries, Leo, and Sagittarius) won't find the extravagance they seek in Pisces, as Pisces is far too down-to-earth to suit them.

Their opposition is such that it could be compared to fire and ice, but in the end, the flames always manage to overcome the ice cube, which in the end only remains a thin puddle of water ...

Virgo: your ideal vacation according to your astrological sign

What is your ideal vacation? Where to go this summer? Where is the best place to recharge your batteries? Do not let chance choose your fate: our astrologer, Chris Semet, gives you all the elements to determine the place and the precise date of your next vacation ...

Sign of the earth, ruled by Mercury (practice, modernity) and Ceres (harvesting, fields, agriculture ...) green landscapes, green or autumnal forests, large expanses of fields, meadows, cottages revitalize you and perk you up.

Your preferences therefore go to hilly regions and countries where flora and fauna are rich. Temperate climates are your preference and you will feel at home in a region mixing land and water, woods and marshes, sand and sea.

Fleeing the crowd, you opt for calm and you like secluded places where you can relax quietly. Your key words are therefore serenity, harmony, fertility, purity ...

Vacation spots for Virgos:

Touraine, Mayenne, Aquitaine Basin, Charente, Vendée, Limousin, Flanders, Picardy, Belgium, Scotland, Ireland, Sweden, Austria, Canada, Polynesia, Marquesas Islands, Seychelles, Réunion, Cape Verde Islands ..., Nepal, Bhutan, China, India.

You don't like the unknown and you can't conceive of everyday life without comfort, so just like your sidekick the Lion, you prefer hotels or seasonal apartment rentals.

Bad habits in couple astrological signs

Love compatibility can be studied in astrology. Thanks to the stars, we can know how it works in a couple and the faults on which we can work according to our astrological sign and that of our partner.

Astrology can be a great way to answer love questions. Whether it is love accounting or advice in a couple's life, the stars can provide you with some answers.

The faults of the astrological signs in couple

Discover the little flaws and bad habits that each astrological sign maintains. By spotting them, you can improve yourself and avoid always falling into the same pitfalls.

Aries is a go-getter who always takes matters into his own hands. In a love story, you can't control everything. He must therefore learn to let things flow. Letting go is the key word!

The Taurus is an astrological sign of the element earth: he likes the concretization and the stability. In love, he tends to be overly possessive and jealous. Flaws on which he must work so as not to suffocate the other.

Gemini love to communicate but ... had a hard time getting to the bottom of it. They cannot say the bottom of their thoughts which creates communication problems within a couple. They must learn to be honest in order to move forward together.

The astrological sign of Cancer is afraid of suffering. By protecting himself too much, he refuses to let others approach. He must learn to open up to create a real connection with his partner.

The Leo always seeks to be at his maximum. Likewise, he expects his other half to be on top and has high expectations. It is important that he accepts the faults and weaknesses of the other.

The Virgo astrological sign is very picky. He wants everything to be perfect ... even his relationship! By accepting the fact that there may be occasional disputes and misunderstandings, he will be able to relativize all the little difficult moments in his love story.

Libra loves to communicate, meet new people, and engage in new activities. She has a hard time settling on one relationship and stabilizing. It's important that she stops fluttering when she meets someone who really suits her. The grass is not always greener elsewhere!

Read also: How does each astrological sign face the challenges?

Scorpio has a little tendency to drama ... A relationship without passion? Very little for him! Yet living in a checkered relationship is exhausting. Roller coasters over the long haul is not sustainable. It is important that he realizes that arguments and impossible loves are not fulfilling in the long term.

The Sagittarius astrological sign loves to have fun and make new experiences. Daily life and habits do not make him dream. He flees as soon as his daily life becomes too low-level. He must learn to appreciate the comforts of everyday life and to stop chasing after a life of fun that will only lead him to loneliness.

Capricorn tends to always put their professional life before their personal life. He should not neglect his relatives, and the person who shares his life otherwise the latter will end up getting bored.

Aquarius often tests their partner to see if they are genuinely attached. By learning to open up and trust, he could have nice surprises in his love life.

Pisces are often undecided. They are unable to make decisions, especially in their personal life. Whether it's hesitating between two people, whether to stay or leave their partner, to commit or not ... they must learn to make a choice and stick to it in order to find happiness.

Your sexual attitude according to your astrological sign
You might not know it, but your zodiac sign has a big influence on your libido. Have you ever wondered why you are enterprising in

bed or why you are the queen of Kamasutra? Here is the answer. You may be surprised. To be taken with humor, of course!

Aquarius: sincerity above all

You are independent and confident. So, faking an orgasm to spare a guy's ego, very little for you.

You don't see what the point is. You just prefer to teach your partner how to make you cum.

You also get bored very quickly. So, if your one-night stand is only missionary, you run away.

What amazes your partner the most is how quickly you get dressed when it's over.

The thing you least like about sex: making taste buds, cuddling after sex.

Pisces: you are intuitive

One thing is for sure, you know a lot about sex! You are sensitive, generous and as you are very intuitive, you know perfectly how to take him to seventh heaven.

Be careful, it is important to give, but also to receive. Don't hesitate to let your partner understand what really gets you off the ground.

What your partner thinks: that he is lucky to have you.

The thing you least love about sex is when he has an orgasm you don't and he falls asleep within two minutes of sex.

Aries: you are passionate

Your ultimate goal: to reach orgasm. You are doing everything in your power to make it happen.

Your partner loves your mentality and likes to try new things to help you reach your goal.

What charms your partner the most: your talents as a gymnast.

What you least like about sex: When your partner takes too long to have an orgasm.

Taurus: you like to do things right and take your time

You are patient and invested in everything you do. Your partners love your dedication and feel extremely lucky to have you.

What charms your partner the most: your divine kisses?

The thing you least love about sex is when you're ready to have an orgasm and all of a sudden your partner changes positions.

Gemini: the queen of Kamasutra

Whether in the choice of partner or sex position, you have a lot of ideas. The problem, you often have a hard time making up your mind. Don't overthink it. Just be yourself!

Because when you finally make a choice, your lovers can't believe it. You are a very good shot!

They love the way you communicate when you want to try something new.

What charms your partner the most: all your sex role plays ideas.

The thing you least like about sex: explaining that you already want to change position after 3 seconds.

Gemini or the queen of Kamasutra!

Cancer: the emotional

It is very difficult for you to have sex without feeling. Very few one-nights stands for you.

What you prefer is to do it while looking the other in the eyes. Even if sometimes you doubt yourself.

You need to know if you're doing it right, if you're the best shot he's ever had. You rarely ask the question openly, but you really would like to know!

People quickly fall in love with you. How could it be otherwise? You are so charming and witty.

But your lack of self-confidence can play tricks on you. So, stop questioning yourself all the time, there's really nothing!

What amazes your partner the most: that you tell them about their ex as soon as you are done having sex.

The thing you least like about sex: going to pee after having sex. You would rather spend this moment in the arms of your sweetheart.

Leo: you have a lot of self-confidence

You love sex, you have a great sex life, and you enjoy being intimate with someone. Your partner returns it to you, he loves to make love with you.

You are always 100% and you like to be recognized. Your great self-confidence is a big asset for giving pleasure and receiving it.

What your partner thinks of you: They feel inferior to you in almost every way.

The thing you least love about sex: not having installed a mirror on the ceiling to admire yourself while you have sex.

Virgo: you don't trust yourself

If your partner doesn't tell you how awesome you have been, you get upset very quickly.

You are moreover a little masochist; you ask him each time his opinion after your part of legs in the air: "So did you like it? How was it? ". You are just trying to improve yourself.

Shy by nature, you take a long time to ask the fateful question. But when you are launched, you are not stopped.

What amazes your partner the most: your knowledge of sex. You are unbeatable, you know everything about erogenous zones, tips for reaching orgasm ...

The thing you least love about sex: cleaning.

Virgo: you need to be reassured!

Libra: the sexting pro

You love to send sext. You are very good at raising tension. Your partner has a terrible desire to make love to you after your ole ole talks.

What your partner loves about you: your perfect command of the French language.

The least favorite thing about sex is having to ask for what you really want. Why can't they just guess it?

Scorpio: you are intense

Everyone feels that you are amazing in bed. But only your partners have the chance to know what you are really worth.

You are sensual without even trying to be, and foreplay holds no secrets for you.

People assume you aren't the type to curl up in your boyfriend's arms after sex, but they are totally wrong.

What your partner loves about you: that thing you do with your tongue.

The least favorite thing about sex is that everyone thinks you don't want to see those you slept with anymore. Just because you're a sex pro doesn't mean you don't have feelings.

Sagittarius: the one that makes everyone crack

Having sex with you is always fun. You have a lot of humor and nothing is ever awkward with you.

You are one of the few who can throw a joke right in the middle without distracting or upsetting the other.

Your energy and optimism make you very sexy. By your side, the others feel like they are the best.

What your partner loves about you: that you are always ready for a second round.

The thing you least love about sex: you're so good in bed that you often have a hard time getting rid of people you've slept with.

Capricorn: the most sophisticated

You like the most expensive sex toys, silk sheets and luxury lingerie. Admit it, you are a bit of a snob. And why wouldn't you be?

The only downside is that you really impress your partners. Even if you don't do it on purpose!

What they take to be condescending is really honesty. But when you find the right person for you, it sparkles.

What your partner loves about you: your lingerie collection. It seems like you've never worn mismatched underwear in your life.

The thing you least love about sex: sleeping in someone else's bed. Normal, you don't have your memory foam mattress, your hypoallergenic pillow and your satin sheets ...

10 signs you're not sexually compatible

Having sex for the first time with someone is stressful. So stressful that the first time is often not the best. And this is normal. But for some couples, even very much in love, in bed, mayonnaise does not take. It has nothing to do with love or attachment, it has nothing to do with performance either. It's just that these couples are not sexually compatible. Here are 10 signs that never fail.

In love, there are those who have found the precious balance between the physical and the psychic.

Then there are the sex friends. They don't want to be together. But their relationship is an irresistible carnal pleasure.

And then there are their frontal opposites: those who love each other and adore their relationship, but who are indifferent to every sexual frenzy.

Here are 10 signs that your relationship falls into the latter category.

You rarely have sex spontaneously.

There is no seduction between you. Falling into each other's arms, jumping on him when he comes home, being late because of a sudden urge... that never happens to us.

Its n 'there is no position that works for both of them simultaneously.

There is always one who appreciates, but never both at the same time. With you, it's each his turn.

You are used to ending up on your own.

Not just from time to time. All the time. Not that it's a bad thing, when you can't do it together, to have a little pleasure alone.

But when spectator masturbation is your entire sex life, there is plenty to wonder about.

The one of you constantly staring into space.

When it's over, the same line falls over and over again: "Oh no! You're done? Too bad, I was just going to get there". Except no. Only the strange stain on the carpet was of interest.

You have sex with the TV on.

You know that having sex against a background of JT is not sensual, but you dare not say anything because you suspect your partner of really watching TV during the act.

And you do too, by the way.

You do the love that 'at the occasion of the holidays or a birthday.

And even in these cases, you do it more out of obligation than out of desire.

You have a big problem with the rhythm.

As soon as one of you starts to really like it, the other makes a fatal change of pace. Too fast, too slow, whatever, all we know is that it ruins EVERYTHING.

You never want to have sex at the same time. Never.

When one is hot as embers, the other is tired / busy / woozy ... All means are good to draw all the excuses not to make love.

Your libidos do not match.

One needs six relationships a week, the other only two or three.

When it comes to sex, he doesn't have a good or bad number of relationships per week. But in your case, there is always one of them who is frustrated at not having their needs met.

And the frustration in the couple is not good.

When your best friend tells you that she always has an orgasm, you don't believe her.

Yet reaching orgasm every time is possible. In truth.

Astral chart: 18 surprises that the stars sometimes reserve ...

It's all well and good the influence of the stars and the moods of Pluto for the Aquarius young ladies, but to be really complete, my birth chart could have added that to the list ...

The Aquarius woman can't get along with the Taurus man ... but she's dating anyway.

Sensitive and dreamy, the native of Aquarius is gifted for the arts ... and in order not to give her any complex, she prefers to let the Taurus man repaint the walls all by himself.

Her number is 7, her tree is pine and her stone is sapphire ... but she likes diamonds.

Down to earth, she doesn't believe in divination ... if she spends her day clicking on magic-voyance.com, it's just for fun.

The Aquarius woman is very attached to her interior ... and she jumps to the ceiling when the Taurus man leaves the hairs of his beard lying in the sink.

Great romantic, she is enamored of strong feelings ... and goes in front of cruel disillusions by choosing a fan of "Mario Kart".

The concordance of Mars and Pluto under the sky of Saturn gives the Aquarius woman a volcanic temperament ... so don't bother her while she watches "Girls".

Keen on cocooning, she attaches importance to well-being ... so she needs to spend a lot of time under a blanket eating chocolate.

Very professional, she likes to work in a team ... as long as you obey her.

Very active, she practices the hula hoop, oriental dance, rollerblading, watercolor and plumbing ... so no, she did not have time to buy the pains au lait.

Aquarius is an air sign ... that's why she missed the pool again.

Calm and discreet by nature, she falls asleep easily ... in the middle of the evenings that bother her.

In love, the Aquarius woman is not inclined to marriage ... well afterwards, if the Taurus wants to break his PEL to offer her a big ring, she wants to discuss it.

When the Aquarius woman is convinced that she is right, no one will be able to change her mind ... and it's really annoying all these people who try anyway!

Her great ingenuity surprises and annoys sometimes ... she's not the queen of Uno for nothing.

Sentimentally, it enchants the natives of Aries and Sagittarius ... Taureans really have an interest in being wary.

The planet that rules her sign is Uranus ... and she doesn't even know where it is.

Eccentric, capricious, nervous, the Aquarius woman is terribly lacking in moderation ... which just goes to show that her birth chart shouldn't be taken at face value.

The astro sexual profile of the sign Taurus

Gemini sex sign Taurus

Are you more passionate like Aries or gentle like Cancer? Discover your love and sexual profile.

Sign of the Earth ruled by Venus, planet of love and beauty, you are in a way a joyful - cerebral.

As a good epicurean, you know how to appreciate all the pleasures in life, even if you don't always seem to be. You cannot conceive of your daily life without love, but you are very demanding.

So, don't become your partner who wants to. Attached to stability, when you are in a relationship, you set up a whole lot of rituals that reassure you.

Taurus in love

You need sensuality and gentleness. So, we can say that you have to be whetted and for that your other half will have to come out on top.

Touch, taste and hearing are senses that must be stimulated for you to reach seventh heaven.

What is Taurus and sex like?

If you like languid hugs, you'll be in for a treat. Thus, with him, the pleasure must rise very slowly to reach its peak and end like fireworks.

Monsieur Taureau under his shy or reserved airs is a real concentrate of "carnal" and therefore sensuality. For him, the longer it is, the better! He never forgets the preliminaries which are for him an appetizer.

The fantasies of the sign Taurus

Nothing very original or extreme. All games with food that whet the appetite are popular Erogenous zones in Taurus.

13 things only Taurus girls can understand

Are you a go-getter with a tender heart and were you born at the end of April / beginning of May? No doubt you are indeed of the astrological sign of Taurus. To help you better understand yourself, we have compiled a list of characteristics specific to the Taurus astral sign.

- **You know how to get out of all situations**

Whenever you have any doubts, you **ask your friends for advice** and they'll look at you like: "What?! Why are you asking us when you already have the solution? ".

Come to think of it, you know they're right, and you end up getting out of this mess on your own.

- **You are a fake callous**

For example, when you are jealous you try to show the opposite. It's one way to **protect yourself.**

You are a strong woman, but sometimes you crack and usually, it's your loved ones who pay the price (we talk about the stack of plates that you broke after seeing your sweetheart talking to another girl?).

- **You are realistic**

People say you are pessimistic when in fact you are just realistic. No question of veiling your face and living in the world of Care Bears. It's not that you see the glass half empty, it's just that you know when to refill it and how to enjoy it well.

- **You don't understand people who go into ecstasies over nothing**

Why go to a party that promises not to be top when you can sit back and relax at home? Honestly, you're not the type to jump for joy over nothing, or show off just in the hope of being seen.

In high school, you were the kind of person to **throw back parties** in the kitchen without worrying about others.

- **You are too demanding**

You only want the best. Your friends are surprised to see you still single, but you explain to them that as long as Mr. Perfect does not show the tip of his nose, you will remain alone. Why settle for mediocrity when you can have the best?

- **You are an independent**

People are always surprised at how resourceful you are. You are like a cat; you always land on your feet. The problem is, you tend to isolate yourself (much like Tom Hanks in *Alone in the World*) and it can get overwhelming quickly.

- **You hide your emotions**

People think you are cold and callous when in fact you are hiding under your shell. At this point, you are worse than Tortank in Pokémon, you could even be compared to Frozen (not the Disney version).

But as soon as you dig a little, you see that you are a real marshmallow, as sweet as a teddy bear.

- **You hold a grudge**

No matter how hard you try to soften yourself up, to forgive or even to forget, you just don't succeed. The moment someone hits you badly, you keep it in mind and are able to pull it out years later.

- **You are generous**

Sometimes you can be close to your pennies, but when it comes to **helping a friend,** you don't hesitate.

- **You are the very definition of the girl who has no time for love**

Frankly, seeing a man tumbling into your house with a bottle of wine and flowers, very little for you. At the limit, you steal the bottle from him to enjoy it around a delicious cold meats board and a series, but it stops there.

You just don't have the time. Between your career, your sports training and your friends, you don't have a minute to spare.

- **You are determined**

Nothing can get in your way. You could lift mountains **to achieve your goal** because you assume that "when you want, you can".

Your friends are in awe of your determination and often take you as a role model.

- **You have your heart on your hands**

Whether you're reviewing a super important file or going shopping, if your friend calls you crying, you run right away.

By Daniel Sanjurjo

www.ingramcontent.com/pod-product-compliance
Lightning Source LLC
Chambersburg PA
CBHW081354160726
48000CB00010B/3348